AF715215

MORE THAN JUST WATER

5 Critical Mistakes Corporates Make While Choosing Bottled Water

MORE THAN JUST WATER

5 Critical Mistakes Corporates Make While Choosing Bottled Water

NAVEEN GOEL

Available on amazonkindle

Worldwide Published by

Pendown Press
PREMIUM BUSINESS PUBLISHER

PENDOWN PRESS LLP

An ISO 9001 & ISO 14001 Certified Co.,

Regd. Office: 3767A, Kanhaiya Nagar,
Tri Nagar, Delhi-110035
Ph.: 8130886000, 9650072927
E-mail: info@pendownpress.com
Branch Office: 1A/2A, 20, Hari Sadan, Ansari Road,
Daryaganj, New Delhi-110002
Ph.: 011-45794768
Website: PendownPress.com

Edition: 2025
Price: ₹ 299
ISBN: 978-93-7217-706-0

Layout and Cover Designed by Pendown Graphics Team
Printed and Bound in India by Thomson Press India Ltd.

TABLE OF CONTENTS

ACKNOWLEDGEMENTS

With deep humility and gratitude, I bow **to *Maa Ganga* and all the sacred rivers of our land**, the eternal sources of life, purity, and inspiration. Their divine flow has nourished not only the soul of this nation but also the spirit behind this work.

I offer my heartfelt *pranams* **to my parents**, whose love, values, and blessings have been the foundation of every step I have taken.

To my *Gurus* and mentors, I remain forever indebted for their wisdom and guidance that shaped my thoughts and purpose.

To my wife, Pratibha, whose unwavering support, patience, and faith have been my strength, this journey would not have been possible without you.

To the joy and light of my life, **my children**, **Pravar** and **Nandini,** your laughter, love, and innocence bring sunshine to my days, reminding me of what truly matters, and your belief in me continues to inspire me every day.

To My Team at Aqueous, Customers, BOD friends and all my friends, thank you for your relentless encouragement, for pushing me to go beyond my limits, and for always reminding me that growth is a journey best taken together.

PREFACE

The Invisible Risk in Every Office Pantry

Every day, employees across corporate India sip from water dispensers without a second thought. As long as the jar looks clean and the water tastes "okay," everything feels safe.

But is it?

Behind the scenes, many corporates unknowingly rely on water vendors who operate without proper hygiene practices, certifications, or testing protocols.

The risk is invisible until it's too late.

I still remember a case from my early career that shook me. A senior executive from an international firm had to be airlifted back to the U.S. after falling critically ill.

The suspected reason? Contaminated drinking water consumed during his visit to a popular heritage site.

That incident, and many others like it, made one thing crystal clear:

Unsafe water doesn't just hurt health; it destroys trust, credibility, and sometimes careers.

In today's workplace,

- HR teams focus on mental health.
- Facility teams ensure ergonomic chairs.
- But **water, the most essential input, is often left to the cheapest vendor** or the lowest quote.

And that's where the problem begins.

You, as the Admin Head, Facility Manager, or Procurement Officer, are the silent guardian of your team's well-being. If the water quality is ever compromised, the complaints won't go to the vendor; they'll land on your desk. Illness outbreaks, sudden inspections, and compliance flags can all trace back to this one overlooked input: bottled water.

Water is more than a commodity. It's your team's daily intake. It touches your people 365 days a year. If it's not safe, reliable and consistent, you're constantly playing with risk.

This book is here to help you eliminate that risk completely.

Over the next few chapters, I'll walk you through the 5 most common mistakes corporates make while choosing water vendors, and how to avoid them with a practical, proven system trusted by leading names like, MNCs, corporates, and multiple government offices.

You'll see how something as basic as a water jar can either cause endless issues or become a solved problem you never think about again.

Let's dive in. **Because this is more than just water; it's your team's health, your peace of mind, and your professional reputation.**

Why Do I Talk About Water With Such Authority?

My Journey from Food Technologist to India's Safe Water Advocate

My name is Naveen Goel (A true-blue, *Chhora Ganga Kinare Wala*), and if there's one thing that has defined my life, it's water.

I wasn't born into the bottled water business.

I was born in Haridwar, beside the sacred Ganga, where reverence for water runs deep.

This reverence for water laid the foundation for my life's mission, and it echoes in my journey.

As a child, I watched pilgrims from every corner of the country travel to take a dip in *"Maa Ganga."* We considered **water not just a utility, but a divine life force.** Perhaps that's where my relationship with water truly began.

After completing my education in Food Technology from the G.B. Pant University, I got my first break with India's first supermarket chain, NANZ. This joint venture between Escorts, Marsh USA, and NANZ Germany offered invaluable exposure to the "farm-to-store" supply chain. During my tenure, I observed that packaged drinking water (notably Bisleri) was the fastest-moving product.

That's also where I witnessed, for the first time, the silent importance of packaged drinking water. One of our foreign executives fell critically ill due to poor-quality water and had to abandon his assignment mid-way and be flown back to the USA.

That incident haunted me. It highlighted the critical importance of ensuring safe drinking water, a realization that steered my career toward this industry.

It made me ask: "How can a country like India, blessed with rivers like the Ganga and Yamuna that are worshipped, struggle so much to offer safe, consistent drinking water?"

This one question pushed me into action.

One fine New Year's Day in January 1996, all this churning and quest in my mind automatically propelled my feet towards the WHO headquarters in Delhi to know more about the impact of potable water and its possible impurities and contamination on a human being.

There, I gained deep insights into various parameters that affect the quality of potable drinking water. From this point onward, I vowed to do something in the field of potable/ drinking water, and I quit my job.

After 3-4 months of research deeply about all the technologies through which water can be purified and made drinkable without any impurities, I entered into the business of Packaged drinking water(PDW) in the 20 litre jar segment to establish **North India's 1st and probably India's 2nd RO (reverse osmosis) based water processing unit,** a technology which had just started to be in use in the United States and Europe. **At the time, RO technology was barely known in India; most big brands hadn't even started using it.**

I named my venture Aqueous Food Technologies and I made it my mission to elevate water to the status of "food" long before the government officially did.

From a 2000 LPH plant, we've scaled to 20,000 LPH today, with two full-fledged units in Noida and Greater Noida. Along the way, I became involved at the highest levels of water regulation.

Over the years, I have actively contributed to the evolution of water standards in India, representing the bottled water industry at forums such as BIS, FSSAI, and CGWA. As the Senior Vice President – All India, of FIPMA (Federation of All India Packaged Drinking Water Manufacturers Associations), I represent over 8,000 units serving 1.4 billion Indians and international visitors. My expertise and leadership have positioned me as a trusted advisor to corporates, RWAs, malls, multistorey apartments, and government departments, enabling them to provide safe drinking water to their employees, residents, and guests.

My journey from the sacred ghats of Haridwar to shaping the nation's drinking water standards reflects my unwavering commitment to ensuring that every individual has access to safe, clean, and reliable drinking water.

Today, I am known as India's Safe Drinking Water Expert.

But that's not what I'm most proud of.

What gives me true fulfillment is knowing that we're trusted by leading names, MNCs, corporates and even multiple central and state government offices. Not just for quality, but for consistency. 365 days, 24/7, zero excuses. Because when you're supplying drinking water, there is no backup plan. No, "we'll deliver tomorrow."

- We test every batch.
- We use BPA-free virgin ISI-approved jars.
- We maintain in-house labs, batch tracking, and real-time site-level delivery monitoring through software.

- We even balance water with essential minerals like calcium and magnesium to ensure the water doesn't just hydrate, but nourishes bones and long-term health.

WHY THIS BOOK?

I've seen **how corporate decision-makers often unknowingly put their teams at risk, just by trusting the wrong vendor** (water partner) or focusing solely on price.

That's why I wrote this book.

I want to pass on everything I've learned, so you don't need to rely on assumptions, sales pitches, or guesswork when choosing the most critical item your workplace consumes daily.

Because once you know what to look for, unsafe water is no longer an invisible threat; it becomes a solvable problem.

And I'm here to help you solve it.

This book is aimed to educate the decision makers at various levels, especially those who make decisions or do procurement, or influence the decision process for one of the most essential and crucial items for the human body, i.e, water. Water is the most important item among all that affects employees' health & well-being while on or off work.

Also, in turn, the appraisal of the decision maker of this essential item is at stake most of the time, and it becomes an eyesore many times with immature decisions. The handbook shall guide them as a lighthouse on how to select and what to look for while procuring the packaged drinking water.

What This Book Will Give You

✓ A step-by-step breakdown of the 5 fatal mistakes to avoid

✓ Practical checklists you can use today and every day

- ✓ Compliance insights that even your current vendor may not know
- ✓ Proof-based systems that give you total traceability
- ✓ An offer to visit a fully automated, BIS-compliant plant, so you can finally see the difference

CHAPTER 1

Are You Carrying the Hidden Burden of Unsafe Water?

IN MOST WORKPLACES, WATER IS TAKEN FOR GRANTED UNTIL IT BECOMES A PROBLEM

Take a moment and think about the last time your team had a complaint about the water supply.

- Maybe the jar arrived late.
- Maybe someone said the water "tastes different today."
- Maybe a colleague fell sick, and no one connected the dots.

But here's a question few Admin or Procurement Heads ask themselves:

"If something goes wrong with the water... will the vendor be blamed? Or will I?"

The honest answer?

It's you.

Because in every office, you are the invisible shield. You are the reason the pantry stays stocked, systems stay running, and people stay safe. But in the case of water, this role comes with a dangerous catch; you don't see the contamination, the compliance gaps, or the delivery failures... until they explode.

Let's get into it deeper:

- You could be working with a vendor who doesn't follow BIS or FSSAI norms.
- Your jars might be recycled without sterilization, or use BPA-leaching plastic.
- The water could have a TDS of under 75, with almost zero minerals, which may be doing more harm than good.

But if something happens, a health scare, a failed audit, or a last-minute delivery miss, the question that comes up is:

"Who chose this vendor?"

This is the hidden burden most decision-makers carry without realizing it.

In fact, this issue has come up in multiple boardroom discussions and internal reviews at the companies we serve.

At one point, a facility head from a global tech firm told me bluntly,

> *"Naveen ji, we just want to sleep peacefully. I don't want a 9 am call saying water hasn't reached any site. And I definitely don't want my CEO asking me why people are falling ill."*

That's when I realized, more than product or price, what decision-makers crave is peace of mind.

And that's exactly what this book is about.

In the next section, I'll show you the **5 critical mistakes corporates make while choosing water vendors**; mistakes that not only risk health and compliance, but your own professional reputation.

Because once you see the gaps, you can eliminate them permanently.

You deserve to never think about water again. Let's make that happen.

What You're About to Discover Could Save Your Team from Harm (and You from Blame)

Let's get one thing clear: this book isn't about selling water; it's about revealing what others don't tell you.

You're a professional; maybe a procurement head, maybe an admin in charge of multiple facilities; someone trusted to keep the basic systems running smoothly. And yet, when it comes to one of the most vital inputs your team consumes every single day, water, the entire industry expects you to choose based on... what?

- A brand name?
- A low price?
- Or just "the guy we've always used"?

Let me show you why that's a risky game.

Why Most Vendors Hope You Never Ask Questions

Over the past 25 years, I've visited hundreds of water processing plants across India, both as a supplier and as a member of the FIPMA BIS/FSSAI advisory panels.

And what I've seen is shocking.

- Plants running without proper licenses
- Water jars rinsed in open drains, not sterilized
- Total Dissolved Solids (TDS) below 20; technically water, but nutritionally zero
- Delivery teams with no hygiene protocols
- Vendors reusing caps, skipping testing, and forging reports

And the most alarming part?

These suppliers are still doing business with big brands, simply because no one has taken the time to lift the curtain.

That's why this chapter is your turning point.

From this point on, you will no longer:

- Be kept in the dark about what to look for
- Be pressured into making choices based on the lowest cost
- Be stuck with vendors who can't scale, can't explain, and can't show proof

Instead, you'll be equipped with clarity, confidence, and control.

You'll see how leading companies, like, MNCs, Corporates and Central Government Ministries have quietly solved this problem by choosing smarter, not cheaper.

You'll learn why your water vendor is your hidden risk, or your invisible insurance.

- No more assumptions.
- No more "good enough."
- And no more being the one who gets blamed for decisions made in good faith, but with incomplete information.

You're about to become the most informed, most prepared decision-maker in your department, and no one will second-guess your vendor choices again.

- This is not just about water.
- This is about leadership.
- Reputation.
- Health.
- Control.

So now, let's enter an important portion of this journey, where we uncover the 5 critical mistakes corporates make while choosing bottled water vendors.

You may already be making some of them.

And if so, let's fix that today.

Mistake #1

Ignoring Mandatory Compliance

(FSSAI, CGWA, and Legal Metrology)

"IF YOUR WATER VENDOR DOESN'T COMPLY, YOU'RE THE ONE AT RISK."

Compliance isn't mere paperwork. It's your insurance policy against disaster.

Yet, in my experience, nearly 7 out of 10 corporates never physically verify whether their bottled water supplier holds the mandatory licenses required to operate legally. Most rely on verbal claims or old scanned PDFs, which could be expired, incomplete, or worse, forged.

Let me break this down clearly for you.

The Must-Have Certifications for Any Packaged Drinking Water Supplier:

Recently, the Government of India has made the FSSAI the sole agency to regulate all food products in India, and in this development, all the food products that were regulated by BIS and FSSAI are now under FSSAI control. FSSAI has formulated its own set of rules to control these food products and put Bottled Water in the High-Risk Food Category, so, as a customer/procurement in-charge, one should check..

1. **FSSAI (Food Safety & Standards Authority of India) License**

   Bottled Water is classified as a food product. FSSAI ensures that proper labeling, hygiene practices, and safety standards are followed during production and packaging.

   FSSAI has adopted the **BIS (Bureau of Indian Standards) rules as of now, for Water, such as**

   IS:14543 Packaged Drinking Water (other than Natural Mineral Water)

   IS:13428 Packaged Natural Mineral Water

   This ensures that the Packaged Drinking Water meets essential safety parameters, including microbiological, chemical, and physical purity standards as per IS:14543

   If no FSSAI License, then the vendor can not legally be allowed to sell packaged drinking water.

2. **CGWA (Central Ground Water Authority)**

   This controls and monitors groundwater extraction. If your supplier uses underground water (which most do), this is non-negotiable. Otherwise, the water could be illegally sourced or unsafe due to industrial contamination.

3. **Legal Metrology Registration/License**

   All the packaged commodities should have Legal Metrology Registration from the weights and measures unit of the Department of Consumer Affairs (Ministry of Consumer Affairs, Food and Public Distribution)

   Now, here's the dangerous part:

   - Many suppliers don't have all the Compliances.
   - Some show you one, skip the others.

- Some show you outdated or revoked licenses.
- Some have only the trading license, not the manufacturing license.

What This Means for You as the Client

You may be buying water from an unauthorized vendor

In case of a compliance audit or health issue, your company could face penalties

And internally, your department could be held responsible for "vendor mismanagement."

Imagine if a staff member fell ill and the water was traced as a cause. You'd be asked,

"Did you verify the vendor's credentials?"

If you can't produce the documents, the blame is on you.

What You Must Do Immediately

- Ask your current vendor for all the licenses
- Verify if they're active and valid; check issue dates & expiry
- Make sure the license is for the manufacturing unit and not for a reseller and it should be a "Central FSSAI License," not one from "State FSSAI."
- Maintain a soft copy & printed copy in your vendor documentation file

Bonus: Ask if they've passed their last FSSAI inspection; most won't know what you mean

At our facilities, we've always led with compliance first, because it's not just about ticking a box. It's about trust, traceability, and your peace of mind.

We welcome any of our clients to inspect our FSSAI/CGWA /Legal Metrology licenses and even visit our plant to see SOPs in real-time.

Because when water is involved, "probably safe" is not good enough.

It has to be proven safe. On paper. On record. On-site.

In the next chapter, I'll show you Mistake #2: a practice that takes just one hour but saves you months of future firefighting.

Let's continue.

Mistake #2

Not Visiting the Vendor's Plant

"IF YOU HAVEN'T SEEN WHERE YOUR WATER COMES FROM... YOU DON'T REALLY KNOW WHAT YOU'RE GIVING YOUR PEOPLE."

Let me be blunt:

If your current water vendor has never invited you to their plant, you should be concerned.

Because what's being hidden... might hurt your people.

Over the years, I've visited hundreds of packaged drinking water plants across India; some are FSSAI certified, many are not.

The difference between what's written on paper and what's happening on the ground can be alarming.

You see, water is not just filled into a jar and sealed. There's a system, a hygiene protocol, and a discipline that must be followed daily.

And the only way to verify that?

A physical visit.

What I've Seen Behind Closed Doors

- Jars are not being washed properly
- Used caps are being reused without sterilization
- Empty jars covered in dust, stacked near the washrooms
- RO filters have not been changed for months
- Storage tanks are not being sanitized regularly
- Workers are not wearing gloves or protective clothing
- Fake testing logs written after delivery, just to "look" compliant

These are not rare exceptions; this is what happens when nobody is watching.

And the scary part is:

Once the jar is sealed, you have no idea what's inside.

You're trusting the vendor to follow safety and hygiene SOPs. But if you haven't visited their plant, how can you be sure?

Why Most Clients Skip This Step (and Why You Shouldn't)

- They think it's "too far" or "not worth the time"
- They assume the vendor is doing their job
- They rely on paperwork or polished presentations

But in water, what's visible is not always the truth.

Even a 30-minute walkthrough can reveal:

- Whether the plant is clean and organized
- Whether SOPs are visibly followed
- Whether workers are trained or careless
- Whether the jars, caps, and dispensers are stored hygienically

And most importantly, whether you'd feel safe giving that water to your own family.

What You Should Do

Request a plant visit with your vendor (if they hesitate, that's a red flag)

During the visit, use a checklist:

- Do they have an in-house lab?
- How are the caps being sealed? Automatically or manually?
- Are they using BPA-free virgin jars?
- Are the premises clean, pest-free, and well-lit?
- Do they maintain batch logs and water testing records?
- Observe real-time operations; not a showroom corner
- Ask to see the delivery vehicle and the jar storage system

Note: *A good vendor will welcome your visit and walk you through everything*

At our plants in Noida and Greater Noida, we encourage plant visits. Many of our corporate clients, from Amazon to Tech Mahindra, have sent their Admin teams to inspect our process, observe live testing, and understand how true 365-day compliance and reliability work.

Because when you're responsible for hundreds of lives, you can't afford to guess.

Seeing is knowing.

And knowing is peace of mind.

Next, we'll expose Mistake #3, the one that almost everyone makes... buying bottled water based only on price.

It's costing companies more than they realize. Let's uncover why.

Mistake #3

Buying Only on Price

"IF YOU'RE CHOOSING THE LOWEST BIDDER, YOU'RE UNKNOWINGLY INVITING THE HIGHEST RISK."

Let's admit it: price matters.

You're managing budgets, justifying expenses, and often under pressure to reduce costs. So, naturally, when three water vendors quote you ₹65, ₹58, and ₹45 per jar... it feels tempting to pick the lowest one.

But here's the truth the water industry won't tell you:

Any jar priced below ₹ 55 is cutting corners somewhere.

And often in ways that can silently harm your team's health or your company's compliance score.

What Goes Into a Real, Safe ₹ 58–₹ 65 Jar?

Here's the breakdown (for 20-litre jars):

- FSSAI-compliant RO purification system with daily testing
- BPA-free virgin jars (costlier than recycled jars)
- Automated capping & sterilization

- CGWA-approved borewell usage and recharge compliance
- Lab testing + in-house water quality control staff
- Delivery logistics with trained manpower
- Tax, compliance filings, and accountability structure

This costs money.

So when someone offers you the same jar at ₹ 45–₹ 50, ask:

- Are they reusing old jars from the market?
- Are they skipping mineral balancing (Calcium/Magnesium)?
- Are they diluting quality by skipping ozonation or using untested borewell sources?
- Are the jars washed manually?
- Are the caps resealed, instead of machine-locked?
- Are they avoiding GST and running an unregistered plant?

Because of that ₹10 you saved?

It could come back as:

- A health complaint from staff
- An HR escalation or internal review
- A failed compliance audit
- Damage to your department's reputation
- Or worse, silently cause long-term harm to your people

The True Cost of Low Price

Let's say your team consumes 100 jars per day.

Saving ₹10 per jar = ₹1,000/day or ₹30,000/month.

Sounds great?

- Now, let's say one day the vendor skips delivery.
- Or the water causes stomach issues.
- Or someone important falls ill and blames "admin mismanagement."

That ₹30K saving suddenly becomes irrelevant compared to the cost of:

- Productivity loss
- Panic escalations
- Vendor switch hassles
- Internal investigations
- And long-term trust erosion

How Smart Procurement Heads Think

Leading corporates we work with have realized one thing:

Low cost without consistency is a liability.

So they use a different framework:

- Compliance first
- Reliability second
- Clarity in the process third
- Price last, but always justified by value

They don't just look at "per jar cost"; they look at:

- Uptime (delivery consistency)
- Traceability (delivery mapping, batch logs)

- Escalation matrix
- Plant visibility
- Health safety assurance

Because they know, it's not just water, it's the foundation of trust in a workplace.

In the next chapter, we'll dig even deeper into safety, and show why skipping regular water quality testing and mineral analysis is Mistake #4... and how that can silently affect your team's health.

Mistake #4

No Water Testing Or Real-Time Test Reports Or Measured Quality Parameters

> "IF YOU DON'T KNOW WHAT'S IN YOUR WATER, YOU'RE GAMBLING WITH YOUR PEOPLE'S HEALTH."

Most bottled water looks the same.

- Crystal clear. Cool. Tastes neutral.
- But behind that "safe" look lies one harsh truth:
- Clear doesn't mean clean. And clean doesn't mean healthy.

Over the years, I've tested water samples from dozens of vendors used by large corporates, and the results were shocking.

Some samples had zero essential minerals, while others were dangerously high in bacterial load, or even contained heavy metal traces.

Why does this happen?

Because most vendors don't test water batch-wise.

- They might test once a month, or worse, once a quarter, just to tick the compliance box.
- They don't have an in-house lab.
- They don't track TDS (Total Dissolved Solids) or maintain Ca-Mg balance. And they definitely don't show reports to clients.

Which means that every jar delivered to your site is a blind bet.

What Real Water Testing Looks Like

A responsible packaged drinking water facility conducts internal testing hourly, daily, weekly, monthly, semi-annually, etc, and third-party lab testing as per the scheme of testing under IS:14543 and as per FSSAI rules covering:

- TDS (Ideal for health: 75–150 ppm)
- pH level (Should be between 6.5 and 8.5)
- Calcium & Magnesium content (as per BIS/FSSAI limit)
- Microbiological safety – no coliform or E. coli
- Ozone sterilization effectiveness, etc, etc.

At our plants, every batch is tested and recorded before dispatch.

Each jar is coded and traceable to the date, shift, and testing log.

We even fortify the water with Calcium and Magnesium, essential for bone health and cellular function.

Because water isn't just for hydration; it's a functional input for your team's performance, energy, and long-term wellbeing.

What Happens Without Testing?

- You may unknowingly serve demineralized water, which strips the body of essential salts
- You expose your workplace to bacterial contamination, especially in summer and the monsoon season
- You risk audit failures if water quality logs are requested
- And worst, you lose trust from your own people if they feel unsafe drinking the office water

One of our clients, a top MNC, came to us after an internal HR complaint flagged "water causing stomach issues." They had been using a "low-cost" vendor who had never shared a test report. When we tested their jar, the TDS was 18 ppm; zero minerals.

It took just 30 days of switching to our process (with mineral balancing and transparent logs) for complaints to disappear and confidence to return.

What You Should Ask Your Vendor

- "Can I see your last 7-day test logs?"
- "Do you have an in-house lab or do you outsource testing?"
- "Do you provide Packaged Drinking Water test reports each month ?"
- "Is your water ozonated or UV-treated? What's the process control?"

If they hesitate or give vague answers, you already know the truth.

In the next chapter, Mistake #5, we'll tackle the biggest hidden issue that causes panic calls, missed deliveries, and unnecessary escalations: poor service structure and no escalation matrix.

Let's eliminate that next.

Mistake #5

Poor Service & No Escalation Matrix

"WHEN WATER DOESN'T SHOW UP ON TIME, NEITHER DOES YOU HAVE PEACE OF MIND NOR YOUR REPUTATION REMAINS INTACT."

- You could have FSSAI-certified water.
- You could be paying a fair price.
- You could even be getting clean, mineral-rich jars.
- But if your vendor misses delivery at 9:00 AM…
- And your pantry runs dry by 10:30 AM…

You've got a crisis, not a contract.

This is where most corporate vendors fall apart:

They sell "bottled water," but what you actually need is a reliable service system.

Let me explain.

The 3 Levels of Service Failure

1. **Late or Missed Deliveries**

   This usually happens when vendors:

   - Don't have proper route planning
   - Don't forecast seasonal demand
   - Work with untrained or outsourced delivery staff
   - Have no redundancy or backup vehicles

2. **Zero Visibility or Tracking**

   You're left wondering:

   - "How many jars did we get this week?"
   - "Who signed the delivery slip?"
   - "Where are the test reports?"
   - And in case of a dispute, there's no log, no dashboard; just verbal back-and-forth.

3. **No Escalation Structure**

   - When something goes wrong, you call the delivery boy. He doesn't answer.
   - You call the vendor owner. He says, "I'll check."
   - By then, your office pantry is dry, staff are complaining, and you're typing up an email that shouldn't need to exist.

The Difference a Service SOP Makes

At our facilities, we've turned water supply into a logistics science.

Why? Because your trust depends not just on water quality, but on predictability.

Here's what that looks like:

- ➢ Route-mapped delivery schedules with buffer time

- Live tracking of jar movement, signed logs, and consumption data
- Real-time alert system for delay, short supply, or staff absences
- Weekly reporting dashboards
- A 3-level escalation matrix:
- Delivery Supervisor
- Relationship Manager
- Plant Director

When your role is to ensure water is always there, you need a vendor who ensures you're never caught off guard.

What You Must Demand as a Client

Ask your vendor:

- "What happens if my delivery person doesn't show up tomorrow?"
- "Can I track my jar movement per site?"
- "Who do I call if there's a short delivery? What's the escalation window?"
- "Do I get monthly service & testing reports for records?"

If the answer is unclear or defensive, you know you're with the wrong supplier.

A Real-World Insight

The Client

A corporate park in Noida with 9 towers.

The Struggles

They had **faced water panic four times in one quarter with their vendor** before they came to us.

Their vendor had

- No SOP
- No spare delivery boy
- And no ownership.

Our Solution

- We mapped their average consumption across towers.
- Accordingly, arrange pre-scheduled replenishment before peak hours.
- And set up WhatsApp-based real-time reporting.

The Phenomenal Result

Since onboarding us in 2022, they haven't had a single escalation related to water.

Because that's the difference between being "just a vendor" and being a trusted partner.

Now that you've seen all five critical mistakes... It's time to connect the dots.

In the next phase, we'll bridge everything we've covered and present two clear paths forward.

- One leads to more of the same.
- The other leads to full control, trust, and long-term peace of mind.

CHAPTER 2

The Cost of Guesswork Vs. The ROI of Trust

"WHEN IT COMES TO WATER, HOPING IT'S SAFE IS NOT A STRATEGY. TRUSTING A PROVEN SYSTEM IS."

Now that you've seen the five critical mistakes, maybe some of them felt familiar.

You might be thinking:

- "We've never asked for test reports..."
- "I don't know if our vendor is FSSAI-certified..."
- "Sometimes delivery is late, but we manage..."
- "Honestly, I've never visited their plant..."

If that's you, you're not alone.

Most Admin Heads, Procurement Officers, and Facility Managers are busy juggling 10 other tasks. And since bottled water is a "low ticket" utility, it rarely gets top attention, until something breaks.

But here's what experience has taught me over 25+ years in this industry:

Water is invisible until it becomes the most visible problem in your office.

The Hidden Costs of Water Mismanagement

Every time a vendor fails, it affects more than your pantry.

It creates:

- Stress for you, handling internal complaints
- Frustration among employees, especially in the summer and the monsoon season
- Interruptions in productivity; imagine a training session, event, or CEO visit with no water
- Damage to your credibility, especially during audits
- Time that could be productively used, wasted on escalations, follow-ups, and vendor replacements

All of that, just to save ₹5 to ₹10 per jar?

That's not a bargain. That's a slow bleed of trust and time.

What It Looks Like When It's Solved

Let me show you the opposite scenario: what our clients experience:

- 100% BIS, FSSAI & CGWA-compliant water
- Tested in-house with reports shared monthly
- BPA-free, mineral-fortified water that supports employee health
- Live delivery tracking; you always know what's been delivered, when, and where
- A service team that's responsive, professional, and proactive
- A plant that's open to client visits, anytime
- A system that just works, so you don't have to think about it

This is the Return on Trust.

You're not just buying water. You're buying:

- ➢ Time saved
- ➢ Escalations avoided
- ➢ HR complaints prevented
- ➢ Compliance secured
- ➢ Your mental peace, knowing "This part is fully handled."

The Two Paths Ahead

Now that you know the truth, you stand at a crossroads:

✕ Option 1: Stay with guesswork

- ➢ Keep working with vendors who "probably" follow norms.
- ➢ Keep assuming quality is okay.
- ➢ Keep reacting to complaints.
- ➢ Keep hoping the next FSSAI audit doesn't ask too many questions.

✓ Option 2: Shift to a Proven, Transparent System

Partner with a supplier who:

- ➢ Shows you their licenses
- ➢ Welcomes you to their plant
- ➢ Sends test reports before you ask
- ➢ Plans deliveries with software, not excuses
- ➢ Offers you a zero-worry water ecosystem

The first path costs less in rupees but more in stress, time, and risk.

The second costs a little more, but gives back far more in trust, credibility, and control.

The question is: which kind of leader do you want to be?

In the final section, I'll share how you can take the first step towards water certainty, with zero commitment and full visibility.

Ready to turn trust into action?

CHAPTER 3

Never Worry About Water Again – Here's Your Next Step

"IF WATER IS YOUR RESPONSIBILITY, PEACE OF MIND SHOULD BE YOUR REWARD."

Let's face it; as an Admin Head, Facility Manager, or Procurement Officer, your plate is already full.

You handle vendor coordination, supply issues, audit prep, employee comfort, and more. The last thing you need is another unpredictable, stress-inducing item on your checklist.

Water shouldn't be one of your daily worries.

It should just work; silently, reliably, in the background.

That's the system we've built.

What We Offer: The "Zero-Worry Water Protocol"

After 25+ years of experience, regulatory membership, and deep work in this industry, **we've developed a full-stack water delivery and compliance solution trusted by:**

- Amazon
- Tech Mahindra
- Blinkit
- Kotak Bank
- Multiple government offices & ministries

Here's how it works:

- ✓ **Plant Visit Anytime:** You or your team can see our hygiene SOPs, jar handling, and batch testing in action.
- ✓ **100% Compliance, 0% Excuses:** We're certified by FSSAI, CGWA, and Legal Metrology, and we'll show you every document upfront.
- ✓ **Test Reports Delivered Monthly:** No guesswork. Every batch is tested and logged. We even share mineral composition and TDS values.
- ✓ **BPA-Free Jars with Batch Traceability:** Every jar is sealed, sterilized, and coded. No recycled plastic. No risk.
- ✓ **Delivery Forecasting & Monitoring:** We use software to track your site's average usage and plan replenishment before you even ask.
- ✓ **3-Level Escalation Matrix:** If anything ever goes wrong (rarely does), you have a clear chain: Supervisor → Relationship Manager → Plant Head.
- ✓ **Proactive Support:** We don't wait for complaints. We prevent them.

What You Can Do Today: No Cost, No Commitment

We offer every potential client one of the following: completely free:

Option 1: Free Water Audit Call

Get on a 20-minute call with our senior consultant to assess your current vendor, test protocol, and compliance gaps. Walk away with insights, whether you work with us or not.

Option 2: Plant Visit Invitation

Visit our Noida or Greater Noida plant. Bring your team. Inspect everything. Walk away with peace of mind.

Option 3: Free Jar Test + Compliance Checklist

We'll test a sample of your current water, give you a compliance score, and show you exactly what's missing, with a PDF checklist you can keep forever.

No Contracts. No Pressure. Just Clarity.

We believe that informed clients make the best decisions. That's why we educate first, sell later.

You've already done the hard part: reading this guide and becoming aware of the risks most people ignore.

Now take one small step.

- ➢ Click here to book your Water Audit/Plant Visit/Free Testing Slot
- ➢ Or WhatsApp us directly **at 9871633255**
- ➢ Or email: **vkabtiyal@gmail.com, naveengoel2050@gmail.com**

Because this isn't just about jars.

It's about your team's health, your peace of mind, and your professional trust.

Let us make water one less thing you ever have to worry about again.

CHAPTER 4

And Don't Forget Your Bonuses!

"WHEN CLARITY MEETS STRUCTURE, DECISION-MAKING BECOMES EFFORTLESS."

Congratulations; by reading this far, you've already done more than most Admin Heads, Facility Managers, or Procurement Teams ever do.

You've equipped yourself with knowledge, clarity, and control.

Now let's give you some tools to take fast, confident action.

First off, here is a quick summary that you can print out & use as a ready reference for easy use instead of referring to the entire book once you've read and understood it.

The 5 Mistakes & Their Fixes: A Ready-Reference Summary

Mistake	What To Do Instead
1. Ignoring Compliance	Verify, FSSAI, CGWA. Check License Validity & Copy.
2. No Plant Visit	Visit the supplier's facility. Use the on-site hygiene checklist.

3. Buying Only on Price	Evaluate total value: compliance, service, testing, reliability
4. No Testing/Reports	Demand monthly test logs + TDS/Mineral data + in-house lab
5. No Service Matrix	Ask for SOPs, escalation points, and delivery forecasting tools

BONUS #1: Water Audit Checklist (Free Download/Print)

Use this before onboarding any vendor:

- Do they have all valid licenses? (FSSAI, CGWA)
- Can they show you their latest test report?
- Do they have a live dashboard or delivery tracking system?
- Are their jars BPA-free & ISI marked?
- Do they sterilize jars with automated machinery?
- Is their delivery team trained & in uniform?
- Can they prove their jar pricing supports real compliance?
- Do they offer an escalation matrix?

Score

✓ 7–8 = Trusted Vendor

✓ 4–6 = Needs Review

✓ 0–3 = High-Risk

BONUS #2: TDS & Mineral Score Sheet Template

Let your internal team or QA team log this weekly:

- Date
- TDS (ppm)
- Calcium (mg/L)
- Magnesium (mg/L)
- Test Passed (Y/N)
- Technician

Target TDS: 75–150 ppm

Calcium & Magnesium: Balanced as per standards

BONUS #3: Sample Escalation SOP Template

Escalation Levels for Service Issues

- **Delivery Supervisor**

  Response time: < 15 mins

  Contact: [Phone / WhatsApp]

- **Client Relationship Manager**

  Response time: < 30 mins

  Contact: [Email / Direct Line]

- **Operations / Plant Director**

  For unresolved issues within 2 hours

  Contact: [Email / Escalation Link]

Final Words

When people ask what you do, they might not realize how many systems you keep running silently.

But trust me, when the water fails, everyone notices.

And when it works perfectly, they forget you had to plan it all.

Let this be the year you take control of the water issue permanently.

Let us help you make it invisible, because it's fully handled.

Your Next Step (Choose One Now)

- Book a Water Audit Call (Free)
- Schedule a Plant Visit (Noida/Greater Noida)
- Request Free Testing of Your Current Vendor's Water
- Download all Tools as a PDF Kit
- Just message "WATER KIT" to **9871633255**
- Or email: **vkabtiyal@gmail.com, naveengoel2050@gmail.com**
  with subject: "Water Peace Pack"

Praise for The Book

"From compliance checklists to moral responsibility —

"Naveen combines experience and empathy in More Than Just Water. His understanding of on-ground facility challenges is remarkably accurate."

Vivek Rajput

Head - Facility Management Services

Delhi International Airport Ltd (GMR Group)

In the corporate world, trust and consistency define every partnership — and Naveen's work echoes that truth beautifully.

"More Than Just Water" is more than a guide; it's a wake-up call for organizations to prioritize quality and compliance in even the smallest daily essentials. I deeply resonate with Naveen's mission, as we both share the goal of creating workplaces that are safer, more sustainable, and built on integrity.

Tamanjit Singh Chadha

Director

Akribiz Business Solutions Pvt Ltd

"Freedom comes with the tag of responsibility. Waterman/Naveen (Modern representative of Raja Bhagiratha) influences his freedom, strength, selflessness, and professional drive, ensuring all dependents are taken care of in all seasons.

Water is essential; I am sure his wisdom on this subject will benefit the next generation indeed. Best wishes for his new venture!"

Guruprasad L

Central Commercial Procurement

Tech Mahindra Ltd.

"This book is more than an operational guide —

"In corporate administration, we often take basics like drinking water for granted.
"Reading this made me realize how something as simple as water management reflects an organization's larger ethics.

Ajay Gupta

Admin Head

BSES Yamuna Power

I've met many business owners and founders, but when it comes to water, no one comes close to Naveen Goel. He doesn't just talk about water; he lives and breathes it. His knowledge of the water ecosystem runs so deep that even experts or Wikipedia can't match it.

When I read his book, "More Than Just Water," I was amazed by how sharply he notices every tiny detail, from water hygiene to its nutritional value. The way he explains complex things in such a simple, relatable way makes you look at every glass of water differently.

This book isn't just about water trust; it's about awareness and health. Anyone who reads it will start caring more about what they drink and why it truly matters.

Shailendra Vijayvergia

MD, Animon

I express my genuine appreciation for the services you are providing. In today's fast-paced environment, where prompt and quality services are the need of the hour, having a reliable partner like you is invaluable.

I wish you more success.

Santosh Kumar

Head Procurement

BSES Yamuna Power

Naveen is a consummate collaborator who believes in building partnerships, prioritizes quality over quantity, and places ethics above all. He champions simplicity over complexity, translating intricate quality concepts into practical, actionable guidance. This book bridges management theory with field reality and provides a benchmark for anyone handling workplace utilities—turning compliance into culture.

Manu Gautam

Vice President & Site Leader (Jaipur)

Metlife

www.ingramcontent.com/pod-product-compliance
Lightning Source LLC
Chambersburg PA
CBHW071400230926
51846CB00002B/609
* 9 7 8 9 3 7 2 1 7 7 0 6 0 *